The Art of Walking Backwards

Other Titles by John B. Lee

Poems Only a Dog Could Love, Applegarth Follies, 1976
Love Among the Tombstones, Dogwood Press, 1980
To Kill a White Dog, Brick Books, 1982
Fossils of the Twentieth Century, Vesta Publications, 1983
Broken Glass, League of Canadian Poets, 1983
Hired Hands, Brick Books, 1986
Small Worlds, Vesta Publications, 1986
The Day Jane Fonda Came to Guelph, Plowman Press, 1989
Rediscovered Sheep, Brick Books, 1989
The Bad Philosophy of Good Cows, Black Moss, 1989
The Pig Dance Dreams, Black Moss, 1991
The Hockey Player Sonnets, Penumbra, 1991
When Shaving Seems Like Suicide, Goose Lane Editions, 1992
Variations on Herb, Brick Books, 1993
All the Cats Are Gone, Penumbra Press, 1993

Forthcoming

Ebenezer the Sneezing Dog, Black Moss, 1993
Dilly Wakeup and the Runaway Head, Black Moss, 1994
Pond Song, Black Moss, 1994
Tarantula: The Riddle Book, Black Moss, 1994
These Are the Days of Dogs and Horses, Black Moss, 1994

The Art of Walking Backwards

By John B. Lee

Black Moss Press
1993

Published by Black Moss Press
2450 Byng Road, Windsor, Ontario
N8W 3E8.
Black Moss books are distributed in Canada
and the United States by
Firefly Books Ltd. 250 Sparks Avenue,
Willowdale, Ontario, M2H 2S4.
All orders should be directed there.

This book was published with the financial assistance of
The Ontario Arts Council and The Canada Council.

Cover art by Tim Dixon
Layout and Page Design by Brian Fox and Kristina Russelo

Printed and bound in Canada by Hignell Printing Ltd.,
Winnipeg, Manitoba.

CANADIAN CATALOGUING IN PUBLICATION DATA

Lee, John B., 1951-
The art of walking backwards

Poems.
ISBN 0-88753-252-7

I. Title

PS8573.E348A78 1993 C811".54 C93-090357-9
PR9199.3.L44A78 1993

Table of Contents

Poems from *The Art of Walking Backwards* have appeared in:

Alchemy, Arc, Breakthrough, BSPS, Canadian Forum, Carousel, Cross-Canada Writers' Magazine, Cross-Canada Writers' Quarterly, CVII, Dandelion, d'Void, Fiddlehead, Grand Memories, Implosion, Kaleidoscope, New Muse of Contempt, New Quarterly, Next Exit, North York Arts Coucil News, The Plowman, Poem Factory, Poems for Sidewalks, Poetry Australia, Poetry Canada Review, Poetry Halifax Dartmouth, Poetry Toronto, The Pom Seed, Prairie Fire, Quarry, Queen's Quarterly, The Shit, Skylark, Tidepool, Toronto Life Magazine, Tower, Twelfth Key, Word Fires and *Yak*

and in the anthologies:

American Poetry Associations' Annual Anthology 86, Anti-War Anthology (Vesta Publications), *Dreams to Dream Promises to Keep* (Northwoods Press), *Great Canadian Poetry Machine* (World's Fair Vancouver), *Peterborough Poetry Festival Anthology, Project Ploughshares Anthology, Speak for Yourself: Listening, Speaking and Thinking* (Nelson Canada), *Surrealism Anthology* (Moonstone Press), *The Train Station* (Plowman Anthology), *and Words of Praise* (American Poetry Association).

"My Alibi for an Eventful Wednesday in May" was previously published in *Love Among the Tombstones,* now out of print.

*"The Days to Come" won fifth place in the American Poetry Associations' Annual Competition for 1987.

**"I Have Much to Confess and "The Day the War Came to Ashbourne, Derbyshire" took eighth place and Second Runner-Up respectively in Cross-Canada Writers' Quarterly competition for 1987 and 1988.

***"The Day I Found Four Score of Starlings Dead in the Franklin" won First Acclaim in the Roundhouse Poetry Competition for 1989.

The Moon Is Never Lonely

...clouds of chalk dust
travel like musket smoke
across the school yard
above the clapped-together brushes
that here and there
have bruised the brick with fans
or left a butter-coloured stain
upon the hands
of the punished boy who snaps them
like the long beak
of a fish-eating bird
or makes them sound
a single gun-crack thunder
so it echoes over the village
or he slaps them lightly
then watches the puff of powder
like the stagy exhalation of breath in the cold.
He marks how each white stripe
comes clean
then goes pollen yellow
if he rubs the felt ribs.
He feels the rough scrub
of their grit on his palm
the extraordinary fluxion of each portion
as he brailles the fissures
and imagines how they have erased
the entire hi/s/tory of his day till then
like death   and time
in the fatal sweep of the teacher's arm.

Is There Anyone Here Can Blaze a Trail

Why not climb to the left of the ladder?
Enough good reasons
I suppose.
Why not sail beneath the water
holding your breath
and steering across the flow
your sail cloth heavy
your topsail cutting the surface like a shark fin?
Why not walk under the bridge
across the river
appease the Troll
smile, perhaps even shake his furred hand?
Why not tip your hat to Curly Howard
and walk into a wall?
Why not strap engines to the elevator
and blast off past the top floor
or drill it below the basement
into the magma lounge?
Why not walk into the furnace
and see who gets burned?
Why not get lost
like a radar blip travelling off the screen
imagining a room full of panicky generals?
Why not burn all your maps
tramp your compass
fill up with blue light
erasing your jet streams as you go
cut loose your co-ordinates
so they drift down like balloon strings
and float away over the city

Events Have a Way

See Mike in the channel
his boat dragged by a dogfish
surfacing and barking like a bloodhound
after bear.
This was the sixties
when I was in a washroom in Detroit city
a frosty carp in a halo of angel fish
toking splifs
their dreadlocks welking
their eyes red with swallowed hooks
their fists dangerous from body music
standing by the urinals
yellow taffy streaks on alabaster
the grates a pool of spawning cigarettes
that die with an ugly hiss
like struck snakes.

This was the sixties
when the Beatles landed laughing in New York
and Murray the K
was fast talking like a train
running over a flattened penny
and the streets of America
were boiling with national guard
and single-minded assassins.

This was the sixties
when Phillip left the county fair
to run from the kitchen palaver
of short-order cooks in a Dresden Greasy Spoon
for Vietnam to blotch his boots in the Mekong
and come to understand that staying alive
is a cruel jest
his brain a stain of alcohol and death.
This was the sixties

when farm boys fell in love with speed freaks
and every river rat with hands
would form a band
and even rich girls with reputations to keep
might drop their pants
and the g's from their participles.
This was the sixties
long before the angry gap-toothed insurrectionists
would cut their hair
and join the chamber of commerce
long before the gagged black boxers
would get too mumbly
for public conversations
long before a certain working-class hero
would die in a mocky drag
while a dough-faced fat boy
sat on a curb catching children
long before we'd crimp and manicure
our perfect money-green lawns
all of us biting our coins
like cynical merchants
all of us
checking our children's diets
and drinking aspartame in our tea.
This was the sixties
with Mike in the channel
riding his small boat like Queequeg
behind a mean dogfish
and me in the washroom
in Detroit unravelling my face, my life in a mirror
like a loose multi-coloured thread.

What Crows Include

A murder of crows
bring their black spoor
to a naked tree.
Corvidae come
to Heckle and Jeckle
a cat corpse
or to ride the wagging opinion
of a cornstalk
and test the rupture of its husk
for the hard yellow meat.

Crow sustains himself roosting on the slender bone
of a branch
his caw-caw
wets the wind
as he salivates
pondering the deliciously moribund vision of death
stropping his bill
against the corky crotch bark
letting his eye slit the horizon
his tongue tintinabulate
like a succulent slapper.

They bring dusk
to the tree with the black foliage
of their feathers.
They bring all manner of ragged shadow
and their song
contains entirety
for crows include the universe
in their singing.

I Have Much to Confess

I must confess
that I understand what Hemingway meant
when he said, "Die, so I can write about it."

I must confess
I do suffer fools lightly
and am troubled by the cruelty
of intelligent humans.

I must confess
an innocence in the face of subterfuge
and that I am an easy mark, a sucker
for the soft sell of hard strangers.

I must confess
I am eclectic in taste
and have few taboos, with a weakness
for Chandler's fallen angel, Marlow
and a passion for Curley Howard
and Johnny Weissmuller's Tarzan.

I must confess
I did not know that Holden Caufield
was sick in the head.

I must confess
I find that the majesty and drama
of the high church
is dull beyond words, except as it breathes in the mind.
and that the drab austerity of low orders
is muck-brown and puffy
with moral mistakes.

I must confess
a bestial fascination
with pageantry and the drums of war.

I must confess
I hate the ideology
of violent folk.

I must confess
I too have pissed brandy into the grass
and clung to people as often
out of jealousy and fear as from love.

I must confess
that the riddle of technology falls apart in my hands
and that I am the kind of atheist
who still believes in God.

I must confess
this unravelling here's as much a surprise to me
as the time my sister
leapt from behind a door
and I jumped out of my skin
pared down to the panic
of drowning things
with nothing to grab at but their own hands
and the water
like grasping at time, sunlight
and the stars invisible on their high shelf
roaring in their vacuum
like a dream.

A Book of Days for My Sister

In the clock-sweet rooms of youth
when we were babes
heroes in pelican-white bundles
clutched in our season
and within the podded hours of our lives
not so much as the slightest rag of a ghost
not the least wee pipe-smoke puff
to frost the clear blue zodiac
of our ticking stars
all that clean steep spring we adored our bodies
though each night fell like a black and windy guillotine
on the headless day before.

We ran around the old Georgian farm house
in the dusk, in the dark
like minute hands by numbered pine stands
our bewildered bell-clock voices
rising like water chimes in a sombre sea of spirits.
Thus all the skipping rhymes
and skirts like bent-over flowers
of girls blooming by the gate
while we boys raced with our spit-flattened hair
the light settled like a cow lying down
in the dew cool sun-killing night
when the summers came and went
like a mother by a half-shut fever door.
And all the winters
that have blown their mob of moments on glass
forget how spring sighs above blossoms
every bird-mad morning
the blood ran the maze of bones
till our time-taught flying muscles
slowed like sleep-thumbed pages
in a book of days.

Lost Long Ago

in his damp trouser cuff
a dime
for a haircut.

Who Maked a Motor?

Mother is humming in the kitchen
like a mosquito under a cupped hand
and I'm her little pre-euphemism boy
my own gases rising
like bread smells
I trail about the house trembling fume.
My mother stops her singing, sniffs,
and politely inquires,
"Johnny, who made an odour?"
Ah, this sweet myselfness.
I am the honeysuckle inside the summer.
It is I who "maked the motor!"
See how it runs, this splendid fragrance.
How could the world go wrong
in the midst of such perfume?

Domestic

My father
on his tractor
turns the field over
like a long corpse.

My mother
in the kitchen
is turning on
the oven
making out
the grocery list.

The window glass
shivers
when the tractor
returns
from ploughing.

My father's face is black.

My mother
has flour on her apron.

The dinner forks
take their place at the table.

They are afraid
of my hands grown smooth
my brain for books.

They too resist
symbolism
by making food
move.

In the Harmonious Kitchens of Christmas

In the harmonious kitchens of Christmas
womb-warm with what ovens do
and alive with the talk of women
smoothly rippled like coffee cream in the air
one aunt romancing the turkey with a spoon
of its own juices
another is stirring gravy on the stove top
a third is looking through cupboards
for spices, doors opening and shutting
like the Marx brothers in a hotel hallway
while mother unstructures the squeaky footstool
and climbs to hand down drinking glasses enough
teetering from the comfortable vertigo of the top shelf
one, two, three, four, five, six, seven, etc.
turned over as if to listen to secrets through tables
huge stethoscopes for the heartbeat of footfalls
or conches for the bloodrush of an inner sea.

Is it nostalgia to remember
how they stood in the perfume of what they cooked
extolling the virtues of aprons
and telling the domestic biographies
of those they loved most
clapping their quilted oven mitts
and rocking on their heels with whipped potatoes
billowing in the pan as if they carried clouds.

In the complicated dance step of preparing a meal
clutching cutlery to their breasts
like dangerous silver bouquets
answering the chime of something done
believing the huge irreversible comedy of the day
while in the sweet rum-coloured sunlight of the cold landing
they click with food

pleased by the comforting insanity of the final rush
for the table
or the afterfull sudsing hubbub of dishes
with uncles so stuffed
they sit patting their bellies like split-seam pillows
half expecting feathers to puff out
between shirt buttons.
Fat men plucking their wattles
and talking of horses.

Tonight when the house is quiet
it will remember nothing.
The bones will settle together in the trash
the grease congeal in the pot
and the table scraps will amuse the country dogs
avoiding sleep long enough
to smack them down
stealing a poultry thigh and
beating their jaws like pruning shears
on a tough branch.
And snow might fall in moonlight
like angels coming back from holidays.
While God is somewhere
putting the kettle on
for all the women who have ever lived.

The Man in the Field

The man in the field
stands in the waist-deep water
of wheat
feeling it sway against his hips
like a woman sweeping her skirts
in a sweetheart dance.
The man in the field
watches the sun solve a puzzle of apple branches
in the slow shake of an easy breeze.
Sees in the drift of acres
how a butterfly comes loose
from the design
and then drops again into the huge yellow pool
of things
like a stray button that follows
a slack thread
from the needle's source
to its place for the first and second stitch.

The man in the field gazes out where the dog is drowned
and leaping above the flow
looking for mice to kill
out where the bees harmonize
and swish on their fuzz
to waggle down the bead length
where the hulls knock together in a beard
like the boots of jewels.

Everything there is to know about the world
is known by the man in the field,
but when he speaks
the wind carries his words away
to whisper in the knotholes of the barn

without so much as touching the boards
and his words stay inside forever
with the hay on the bottom
like memory.

The Confrontation

My father
reached in through the car window.
Reached in with his voice
calm and stretched out
like a tired man in a bath.
Reached in with words
rhythmless as a tap running a tub full
slow and easy and tepid.
Reached in to where
the scrawny drunk
was strangling Murray
holding him down on the front seat
and choking him, slowing his breath
to choppy little gulps.
And my father
just eased his voice along his arm
slacking it to the fingertips
as if he were just calling off a dog.
And Murray
rolled out from under the bastard
alive and startled by it
took a swig
from the whiskey thermos on the floor boards
and that was that.

There's Nothing Like a Shade Tree in a Field of Grain

When all my verbs are tense
and sun beats hard within my head
like the heart of a time-worn man
climbing his last on a set of stairs
I know it is the hour
to put all work aside and rest
and then I think
there's nothing like a shade tree in a field of grain
to soothe these tired bones awhile
beside old Tom, the hired hand
who sits like a stubbed-out cheap cigar
in that shade
when the field is cut
and another jag is waddling
up the cow-clut rutted lane
for the barn.

Far from the thresher's noise
we're pitched like culled sheaves
our bodies lost
in soft grass
the heat
gone dizzy in the distance
where it shimmers like whiskey in the brain
and the kind of silence
you can not, will not
fill, comes on
when birds are still
with listening.

The Prosperity of Plums

The plums dropped
one by one like plough horse dung
in the blue orchard
soft as the underside
of a girl's new breasts
and we'd lie on the hummocks
and fling the pits
like knackers in the grass
where the bottle flies
erased the thread of fruit
left wattled on the nut
by the incompetence of human teeth.

Soursweet as bad romance
under the tree
that spun with birds
who circled like satellites
the high horded prospect of the crop hooked
deliciously beyond our reach
where wind strummed the loose-stringed lute
of the branches
or knocked a music through the heavy cargo
where the caterpillars
munched and arced on the vault of leaves
like the eyebrows of Groucho Marx
looking down the front of a buxom starlet's dress.

The Muirkirk Mill

The Muirkirk mill was aromatic
with molasses
and the men stood some, their teeth tawny with chaw
swished and spit
on the slickered floor
while one
slim in granny glasses
and gullet like a knot in barn rope
smoked a roll-your-own
waiting while the grain was bagged
so it huffed
like a fat man's corpse
onto the trolley
and wheeled across the skip of nail heads
to the truck
then pencil stubbed
by school-boy calculations
ciphered slow and sure
on the slip pad
and we were "yupped" away
so the tailgate flacked down
clacking on the weight of its joints
slapping metal in the rain ruts
of the yard
leaving behind the roar
of the huge & hungry engines
where the mill men stood in doorways
lime-white with the work
their khaki trousers clapping
in a cross breeze
ghosted with dust.

The Days to Come

I love the way the world works.
The way a June morning
can hoist its flag of honeysuckle smells
over the yard
owning every molecule
from here to star life and back
how it wakes with birdsong
that lifts the silence from the grass
like a fragile kite
and how light soaks through tree branches
like amber wine
and how the slow and solitary voice
of a milk cow
can drift across the pasture
like a coffee smell.
I love the clack of a wooden screen door
letting children out and in
through the slanting hubbub
of breakfast sounds
or how the morning talk
across a table
can make or break a day
the life till now like a puzzle
finished and carried across
a level room
the way the space between souls
closes just a little then
within the safe circle
of hearts alike we almost believe
we'll surely improve the days to come.

Hear How She Brags

Her father is a nuclear physicist.
Can't you tell by her own high brow?
Can't you tell by the yolk
leaking from her ears
the froth of whipped albumin
at the corners of her mouth
she is an egg head
who likes her men hard boiled.

Her hair has the unpaid-for look
of all misunderstood genius.
Her father came in his genes
intact in microscopic flecks
he climbed her double helix
like a flea circus.
Fashioned the exact angle of her beak.
Chiselled the starved look about her eyes.
Sprung her ribs like a cooper.
Set her organs in their slush.
Put an end to her smug ovum's doomed autonomy.
Made Mr. Wiggly Sperm's
yclept selfhood
throb through the pink oven
beyond her mother's underwear
and then and there she came alive
like a stroked cat.

Ah, what serendipity!
Her papa a nuclear physicist
on intimate terms with the universe.
The mauve-skied hugeness
of his intellect
arcing over her cradle.
No coal miner he. No farmer.
No mugwump.
No, he's a veritable crowd of brains.
His acumen sprawls
across the riddle of the Sphinx
as if it were a Wednesday evening grocery list.

Poem for the Declaration of Feet

How many people
we've loved
and yet never to have seen their toes.

Their hands dangle
like children naked in the rain
their faces
bare
yay, even to glimpse betimes
the uvula
wagging in its inner tunnel
like a gargled bit of meat.

Such countable intimacies of teeth
  such necklines
such plunging billows such jointed revelations
  from knee to calf to wrist.
But the feet
hunkered in their hard shells
like shiny beetles under tucked-down wings
  where the arches
splinter to an artful splay of toes

night crawling in their dark sleeve of socks

with nothing to do but hide
and bear their burden
of loneliness.

I Hear There's Money in Basketball

for Aaron

This small blond boy
thrashing about in the pool
like a kitten
in a cattle trough
knows already
that life often
ledgers its zeros
to the left of its ones.

That cops get shot
through their uniforms
and firemen burn in their boots
and cowboys
die dreaming with their pained bones
jigsawed inside the flesh
and soldiers
scatter their atoms
like a sneeze
in the quick rebuke of souls called war.

So, when he's asked
what he'll do with his life
he says,
"I hear there's money in basketball."
and leaves it at that.

Waitresses

Good waitresses are the heroes of my world
keeping our orders
in their heads
like verb declensions in some arcane language.
Bringing us too much booze
and angling in our bone mess
like micro surgeons.
They hover Valkyries
over soiled dinnerware levitating ash trays like
resurrections.
They come to us juggling coffee
and dainties and flaming ouzo
in a pinwheel pattern
smiling as if each meal were our own private
huki-laou
and they offer the bill finally timidly
their own poetry.
We read, impressed by the line breaks
the way it all adds up
and the strong finish
as if the last line were always,
"Thank you. Have a nice evening."
As if we were royal
instead of drunk and trying to make
the last train connection before shut-down.

Consider the Roofers

Consider the men walking on the roof
across the way
like mountain goats
they lean into gravity
hang in the very air
spiked to angles they list across rain gutters
clutching shingles
biting a row of nails
and talking like bad ventriloquists.

Consider the poet
struggling to unmumble their essence
in a line
the way their hammers fall
the way they fix a shingle
cock their caps
or slide and glue their prostrate bodies
to a dangerous geometry.

Consider how he sits
and watches
knowing they will never quite walk past the edge
nor leap to the fickle gravity
of his page,
but if he shoves them
they would drop to the ground
a very harvest of roofers
and if he wills it
they could vault into the sky
brandishing their hammers
grasping an invisible web of vectors he has strung
especially for their sky dance.

Consider how he sits now
having finished with them

how they work on
as if they hadn't died this morning
or as if their mad flight across the city
were de rigueur
for roofers.

The Wind Storm

summer breath shook first each tired leaf
as if it were a friendly hand
within a crowd of easy votes
then came splashing sudden rude
a clash of tumbling cats
and all the tree limbs
danced with rain
that riverred down the air
like a hundred-fold of clumsy drunken grooms
while here and there
                    a branch
unhooked and flew
spearing a whirl of dizzy grass
or scissored
like a broken kite
clapping its futile green applause

then just as quick as tumbled dice are still
a quiet came
to hush the lawn
like horseman's felt
and we who saw it
whispered how the afterlight was soft
as ointment
in a nurse's palm
salved upon the healing day.

Tonight it Rains

Tonight it rains
and the rain is hopping in the street
like fleas jumping in carpets
a week away from the hound.
Nothing but gardens
feeling the dark and deep resentment of flowers
for heavy weather
their petals drooping like hatbrims
of Harper Lee's southern Belles
warding off the heat
in the mature lattice-work light of an afternoon.

Even an hour since the decline
the trees are dripping
like the tongues of drinking dogs
and all the husbands but me
are sawing at the bedposts
with the satisfied snores of those who labour
while a hundred weeds grow wise in the undemocratic academy
of water
needing tomorrow to be pulled like boat anchors
from their roots
or like hooks from the mouths of fish
who swallow too deep
and die.

This Broken City

I live in a broken city
where a factory falls
brick by brick
like bruised and windy apples
and there are such unbuildings
as were known in the war-torn strasses
of Berlin
single-walled unstructurings
that shave a fractioned square
of madly de-architectured space
flecked with a wash of white
like crumbled lime
and here and there
a bit of blue light
punctures where a block
unmortered worked a mortal window
unintended
gaily dismantled in the residue
as if a hundred smokers
flicked their ash and took the fire
with them where they went.

More than once I stop
to contemplate
the empty store fronts
indecorous with plywood
where a showy garment should have been
while some punk declares his lust
or bangs his head
in time with rhythms
only dogs can hear
beneath the pops and whistles
of traffic
while the day decays
in bloody rainbows

over the death rattle of the Grand
piano of the river.

Cottage Fall

I marvel at the extraordinary kitsch
of certain cottages
the accumulated gimcrack of ugly lawns
green pinwheel enthusiasms
that spinning mark the gravel drives
false blooms aligned and stuck
like fifteen antebellum virgins waiting to dance
butterflies nailed to turquoise boards
like barrettes in the frozen hair
of big-boned brides too cheap
to hire a comb.
How people loll in chairs
the windy pages of large books
fluttering in their laps.
Between fawns and lambs
and swans and loons
windy geese and tacky tall flamingos
and cartoon cats churning on stakes
like the legs of children
startled into the air by tall men—
how dare we strive to decorate
this big blue world
when apples turn and blush in branches
as if the sun were a whispered indiscretion
in the leaves
and chicory and queen Anne's lace
consume the ditch with colour
and holly hocks evaporate with bees
humming in their bells
like boyfriends gone courting
with rings in their pockets
such a brief religion is the early fall
when trees begin their flirting
and all the birds are married.

The Weeds of the Field Were Waving

The weeds of the field were waving
like lust in a straight jacket
and all the birds
had strings.
The crickets were busy
as Arab women mourning the dusk
and every pigeon shuffled the rafters
of rattle-trap barns
like men who had changed their mind about suicide.
The lake was rolling its coins
beyond the cliff, the blue house
was hiked on its skirts
looking for mice
and fall was coming like Fuller Brush down a dusty road.
How could we walk in memory as thick and slow
as dream running
when summer was a river slowed by branches at a bend.
Women were weeping like flowers after rain
and the ships were sailing above their anchors
hooked in the sand
like the ribs of drowned sailors.

Driving North from Weybridge

Driving north from Weybridge
into a juggler's horizon
that lay beyond
the gray-green
army-coloured hills
rolling away like a man's knees
under a blanket
—on the left hand—the sun
like a ripe Cedar Springs peach,
—on the right—
a gooseberry moon
considering the season of her shallow tides
like the walking flux of a slip
too long for a hem...
driving
while daylight dims
softly caught by its own slow gravity
like the slide of soap
on a dishwasher's glass.

November Ditch and the Pasture Beyond

Ditch pods nod
like sleepy readers
where the black dog's tail
thumps the grass and gathers burs
or where she nips herself
plucking pitchforks from her matted coat.
All afternoon
the fieldmice skitter and disappear
their bellies fat with fall
while squirrels chitter and pause
to solve their nutshells
rolling them like monochromatic Rubics cubes
in tiny rat hands
then jumping stuff-cheeked from broken fence to leafless branch
that wag and wave each like a boy
saying goodbye to summer.

Only weeks ago
we swam the meadow blooms
where colour spread
like butter dropped in boiling water
but now there is a brownness undenied
where the smothered sun
must struggle
to lift a single hue
a variant of brown
an alternate gray
as if some artist
blinded by dusk had pooled his bleakest drams
and dipped his brush in silt
or rubbed a pencil's edge against the sky.

Poem for the First Tree to Turn in My Street

There is one tree on my street—
the first to catch pale fire
the ghost of flame within each leaf
returning slow as evening falling early
in the cool-breathed afternoon
that etherized them one by one
unfitting from the puzzled branch
addressing an autumn that's come
for my children
bounding home
under streetlights that aggrieve the passing day
like parlour lamps upon the print of some sad book.
Too soon there is no time
with the slowing pulse of footfalls
fading deep in the breast
of some faraway hill.

Today on My Walk I Thought

Today on my walk I thought
"How clean my neighbourhood."
This man's lawn
groomed like a liberty-ball marine.
That man's house
shingled straight.
Those windows there
smoothed with light
the gutters streaked with car wash
the birds
rehearsing like church sopranos
a matin
everything squeaky as bathtub feet
while a chef's best-butter sun
spilt through clouds
white as a milk-drinker's teeth
in the minty grass-cut air.
Then I could have circled the earth with my arms
and squeezed
it like a visiting daughter
but the bus stop made
its nasal honk
coughed a cook-smoke puff of dirty exhaust
and carried the city away.

Why Women Don't Wear Girdles Any More

Watching you dress
I notice
your shape
perfect for your slip and skirt.
The soft roundness
which if you wore a girdle
would demand I call you
Delores or Gertrude or Grizelda.
Straining into a rubbery exo-skeleton
like the berthing of a turtle.
Your buttocks vulcanized.
Your tummy slabbed plumb
like a trowelled wall.

Pity our mothers
plaited and squeezed
into the cruel geometry of their fashion.
Pity our fathers
dancing against the sad reptilian truth
of case-hardened lingerie.

Blinded by Orchids

I am here blinded by orchids
in the swooning veils of your flesh.

Sleep is a story I will not tell tonight.

For all the coin in this city
I would not miss
this single cloud
that strays like pipe smoke across the heavens.

I will lie awake
till the dawn-bruised sky
flexes its four horizons
and the dogs gone lonely
in their far hills
melt home.

Origami

I watch her
where she folds
in the laundry room.

To me a sheet
is a bulky
hide and seek of hands
a shirt
slumps into a crooked heap
a knocked down mutter
of cloth
and a pant crease
slashes all angles
like crumpled tin along the trouser line.

But for her
it all whooshes and settles
into a wonderful plication
like the backwards footage of an explosion.

For this I imagine the complex origami
in the womb.
This making of girls.
This making of women.

Ideolove

Ideology is for idiots.
Give me love.

I have nothing for strangers
except my love for my friends.

This is not another kind
of xenophobia.
I am unafraid of strangers.
I will talk to them.
There is no percentage
in always suspecting guns.

But my heart is already crowded with affection.
My greatest work
is an embrace for my children and my wife.
My arms make a tiny circle
where there is no room for the world.
The world would break my hands apart
a dissipation too thin to breathe.
It would make a most unenriching and intellectual broth
fog on a landscape at noon
the etiolated sun wan, insipid and lurid
by turns.

Yet many delicate circles touching and thereby
braceletted form a most gorgeous and
natural harmony
where love is the same within each
whole and radiant and sufficient
unto itself.

Snow

The art of snow is in the winter air
And grieving white along dark branch's black.
The cold is resting like a leopard there.
It waits to fall upon a wind-flicked back.
And all the sky is full and ripe with pelt,
A blanket shook to fuzz a strife of light.
The softness lands and there begins to melt
Or freeze within those brittle arms of night.
The moon is lost and likewise are the stars.
The houses sit with candled window panes
And passing up the road, our moth-lit cars
While late night goers struggle up their lanes.
The smell of snow is like the smell of death.
Two lovers meet and die without a breath.

Man Hit By Goose

So when the goose fell
like a huge hunk of angry rain
its beaky nemesis scored
a sudden silence
on the man from Tennessee
who heard the applause of a cluster
of pin-pricked balloons
crowded into an instant
when all the colour shrank to a single
withering wafer of black
shook-out like a wind-snapped sheet
and he was gone
a stone-dumb lump in the boat
behind the blind
a red gash opened a tightrope of blood
on a forehead crease
where his heart teetered
like a fat little clown.

Above him
the brothers honking like a traffic jam
going south along the skyway
laughing
at the rough justice
gathered around the nightly pond
for they have always known
life's as easy as laying eggs
in a refrigerator.

The Day I Found Four Score of Starlings Dead in the Franklin

The day I found four score of starlings
dead in the Franklin
the living room smelled
like a pigeon coop.
We'd been away for the summer
and they'd flown
down the flue
and been trapped there
beating their black wings blacker against creosote
then finally falling to form a heap
the bottom birds crusted and stiff, long dead
each one flat like a crushed corsage.
The top birds
some still warm, still full of what it meant to fly
to hold the sky
beneath them like a nest.

And afterwards I climbed the house
to fix a wire grill
above the hole
while the starlings circled anxiously
as if I were sealing off
their last passage of escape.
As if the chimney were a tunnel
they'd dug
to get out of the world.

Canadian Spring

And this is March.
And it should not be snowing .
Girls should bring their white legs to the air.
Should shorten their skirts
with needles in their lips
and skirling hips
should swing about the streets
arm in arm
unbundled and spilling terpsichorean scales
their flesh alive and brave
enough to choke old folks
and make them spit warm tea
into the crocus beds.
But this is March
when the nicotine sun is hiding in an immoral sky.
And it is snowing.
Two girls walk by
this poet's window clogged in heavy coats
scarves about their throats
talking over a mathematics problem
investing their desire in a chance encounter
with some unconforming fire.

A Prayer

Thank God
I have not grown used to things.
Your hand
on my neck
is still an adventure.
Morning sunlight exploring covertops
is a dog
with its nose on the forest floor
and when I touch your flesh
it is something rare.

I am the child
of an animal
thank God.

I have not grown used to things.
Thank God
I have not grown used to things.

The Song of a Husband in Love

What an exquisite organism you are!
What a specimen!
A lovely primate with all those wonderful
woman gadgets.
An inhabited fecundity.
And damned smart.
Wise as water.

At night
when you slide
like the last of the jam in the jar
into sleep
I lie beside you feeling how you warm the bed
leaving a fever in the sheets
even after you rise
or listening to the moon-tides of your breathing
I feel in you
the pleasure of fertile ground.
One seed. One earth. One summer. One flower
blooming better than a hundred books
planted deep in the mind.

But Can You Dance to It?

When every new mystery is paid for
then the jukebox plays our song which is:
like bullets falling from a box
onto a kitchen counter
like a bag of sea shells
dragged across the hood of a car
like a woodpecker
punctuating sheet metal
like a cutlery drawer
dumped into a roast pan
like a bee hive pulled
through a key hole
like a vice tightened
on a light bulb
like a cat climbing blackboard slate
like someone high-diving
into an empty pool
like a train load of pigs
derailed and plunging into a shallow river
like a dog with a marmalade jar
stuck on his snout
like a live chicken
being sawn in half with a steak knife
like the mighty Kong
squeezing pianos
like someone hitting you in the ear
with an egg
like someone hitting you in the ear
with wind chimes.

My Alibi for an Eventful Wednesday in May

I am lost in a room
where we did not meet
listening to the song
that isn't ours
thinking the thoughts
I didn't think
when we didn't meet here.
I don't remember
what you didn't wear then.
I think
it wasn't pink.
I don't recall
what you didn't
whisper in my ear.
I think it wasn't spring
when we weren't here.
I don't remember the carriage
that didn't bring us here.
I don't remember
not kissing you
after we didn't drink champagne.
All that I recall
is that the nude
who didn't dance
on the table
wasn't you.

Before Death There Is: Still Life

When Dali was severely burned at a party
already in his eighties
he finally wished
for death
but we are what God pretends
so He lit up
Salvador's body
like a stagy cigarette
then snuffed him half-smoked
suspending the agony
of propped open windows
in his flesh
the screak of light
scritching through glass to get at a wall
the scribble
of half-inked nibs
against nerve tips
and before the hours go
they must all tick one by one like slow coins
rolled first down the long branch of his bones.

The Hollow Dark

Sorrow can break even
this big man
gentle as old Cloudburst
my father's prize bull.
His arms hang like heavy doors
that drag his shoulder hinges down.
All the rippled rib slats
whinny under his shirt
to the half breaths
as if he'd starve himself for air
and the large hands dangle from his coat
like shook-out roots limp &
withered three days composted in the sun.

But its the eyes that worry
eyes that look too closely at the world
as if every face
had invisible slivers of mystery
he needed to pinch
and scrutinize.
The eyes uncentred and flooded
with mute moments
like the dampered sounds of a hammer
in a distant room.

A friend noted how this man
would focus on words
coming from a mouth
look at them strangely
turning their facets in the air
so even the simplest message
would come in radiant complexities
uncomprehended, infrangible
disconnected...
he was like a dog in front of a barking television

all that sound all that sound
reaching in and stirring
at the hollow dark.

Tanka on Faith

I breathe because I
believe in breathing, and I
have a kind of faith
in life. I hear my beating
heart:a closing rose . . . o p e n s

A Story

To see your father drunk.

To have him clench you in his arms
in this embrace
for strangers.

To have him place his cheek
against yours
his breath like uncapped cleanser
his words of love
a slurred song for hookers
and fallen priests

his dumb laugh
like spilled whiskey.

To have your father merry and garrulous
as a girlfriend

suddenly turn dark
so something travels from his brain
to his fist.
Some mad commuter in his blood
that straps his fingers to a hard curl
that makes him bring his weapons
to the kitchen.

With you gathering and counting
your teeth
like pearls from a yanked necklace.
He strikes
bent and weeping
your sobs luxurious
he spins you
like a reckless dancer.

You see your father drunk

but he has the delicate hands
of an artist

and you walk with him
along a grassy river

as he speaks to you
the charmed sky is breathless with light.

He holds you
though your head is shaved
like a bad French girl's.
He holds you
though you have betrayed your entire village
by loving him.

The Day Lenin's Ear Fell Off

for V. Mayakovsky

The day Vladimir Ulyanov Lenin's ear fell off
he was listening to the stars.
Under a stupid glass sarcophagus
in the heart of Soviet Russia.
Under the humourless ideology of tourists
his ear fell off like a loose pyjamas button
and rattled silently to the coffin bottom.
An amazing bit of cosmic terrorism.
The sluggish Karma
of an ear lopped off
by the slow rot of time.
How it waited..."seemed i' the air to stick"
gathering force until finally
it made its peace with gravity
and plunked down like a fruitless flan
or leathery fig.

Oh Lenin, lend me your ear.
You must have been very smart
to have made such grand mistakes.

Oh Lenin, lend me your ear
so that I may hear
what you hear
beyond the great engines of inner space
where you may listen
when the heart is truly silent.

Full Leafed We Fall

There is a tree
that looks like a bomb blast.
There is a general
who looks like Mr. Peanut.
There is a president
with wattles like an oven bird.

They have a button
and a red phone
a phone the colour of blood
the colour of halloween devils.
They have targets in mind
targets with strange appellations
Yuri, Cho en, Hey sus, Phillipe.
They have concentric zeroes
diminishing each within each
to a point.

They imagine smoke heaving above a city
like grey blankets over a fat man
restive with flaming ulcers
and bed sores
the size of fifty cent pieces.

They imagine winning
the scorched earth pocked with corpses.
Strong women. Strong men. Pillars of ash.
Weak men. Weak women. Pillars of ash.
An arbour day for planet earth
with upside-down trees
for rakes.

An American Dream-Polemical

They have given the world
a bomb
and a love for money
and a dream of power
and the tyranny of numbers
and talking heads
with the image unfading
and legend in place of history
and figures larger than life
for life is shrinking
and man is serving the screen
and the irrelevance of truth
and the consequence of game shows
and the royalty of performers
and the transformation
of the psychopath
and elevator conversation
with world leaders
and easy revolution
and the instant replay
and round-the-clock sports
and exports like Coca Cola
and fast food and the automobile
and the good news Bible
with a Bowdlerized armageddon
and the seduction of the Sadducees.

Is it any wonder
that they would destroy the world
casually
in abstraction
because it is their world
and they have made it irrelevant
and they would cancel it
like a failing series
like a situation comedy
that no one watches
and no one would miss.

Predicting the Past

...the butterfly folds his wings
and crouches backwards into the sheath of his cocoon
like a flame going out
the gray stub of a final voice
falling into white noise...the dial tone of a dead planet...
..."we are not God...
hello...we are not God..."

A Second Fall From Grace

Once on a long trip
past Iron Bridge
we stopped for dinner
where all of us spied
a deep-dish lemon meringue pie
sitting in a glass case
Oh, and this was a most luscious looking pie
a pie-of-our-dreams pie
a pie-in-the-sky-when-you-die pie
a quintessential pie
a Platonic pie
a floating-in-a-parallel universe
where all-pies-are-perfect pie...

and the waitress took it down
from within the glass
the meringue jewelled with dollops of honey
each of us salivating
each of us lost in a most heavenly
and passionate anticipation.

For the longest while we were
mesmerized by the wedge
that sat on our plates
like a very slice of paradise...

until we lifted the sweet ambrosia
to our lips
and tasted...the bland
corrugations of pasty pastry
the gelatinous ugh
and the rubbery goop
that puddled on our fork tines
like egg yolk.

For an hour after that we drove
our shoulders slumped
our pupils fixed and dilated
as if the pie
were a bad drug we'd taken
as if our belief in roads
were the only antidote
to the brutal nostalgia
of that first taste
of evil.

I Travel by Pencil

I travel by pencil
and behind my eyes
there is a kingdom which sweeps
across he universe
like divine speculation.

What need for armies
gouging the life from houses
like picks poking at nut meat?

What need to surrender
when the will
is as easy as breath
swishing through a sprig of violets
soothing their fragrance into life?

What need for crushing
and killing
when a sea of stars
awaits the dance of a generous mind...
like a lonely bachelor   like a gentle maid.

Some People are Just Lucky

They drown in frozen water.
They choke on supper at a paramedics convention.
They catch on fire
in the bathtub, or in a swimming pool.
They fall from a great height
onto fat pedestrians.
They get dysentery before the big thrust
of a global conflict.
They survive tornadoes
by being at the neighbours for coffee
when their own houses cave in.
They endure the deluge
by owning boats.
They sleep through earthquakes
with the headphones on
listening to the Rolling Stones.
They have their purses stolen
while their keys are locked in the car.
They lose their virginity at sixteen
but find it again at thirty.
They marry wealthy micro-surgeons
with bad eyes but steady hands.

Sometimes
they wish they were dead.

Sometimes
they get their wish.

Where Are the Gravity Police

Sometimes, some of us
fall up.
Always
step past the rim of the canyon ledge
and sweep upwards
through clouds
our shirttails a jet stream.
See us clinging in rows to your rain gutter
holding to it
like blue flame on gas jets
our feet pointing up.
And sometimes
if someone pushes us off a balcony
we might
fly past your open windows
hiking our zippers
with strange expressions on our faces.
You might see us
climbing upside down ladders
perpendicular to the rungs
like bits of cloth
blowing by
our jogging shoes flicking off
like spooked gulls
our hair flapping
in our minds a single thought
the feel of the moonlight on our backs
the feel of the moon.

If I Were a Sheep

If I were a sheep
I would attack people
who wear sweaters.

Plant bombs in their sweater drawers.

Hang around in closets
like an assassin.
Tackle them in the street
like a purse snatcher.

Be a mad and selfless terrorist
bringing death to poets who stare dream-eyed nincompoops
in tweeds from book jackets
or hostesses
who stand slender-legged and bored
on worsted rugs.

If I were a sheep
I'd hang all mutton-chopped professors
by their jowl
like cold meat.

I'd poison the eaters of lamb
by the table full.

I'd have myself photographed
wearing a crisscross of bullets
with a large cigar
clamped in my mouth
holding up the severed heads of children
like a stringer heavy with carp.

If I were a sheep

I'd put an end to hypocrisy.
I'd be strong
and savage your armies
like a hill fighter.
Lean and unemotional
I'd learn your human ways.

In the Heart of a Great Noise

In the weird acoustic shadows of the civil war
close to the thunderclaps of battle
a witness could sit in the silence
like someone dreaming in a room.

All the awful dispatch of the guns
would fall to deafness in those trees and hills
as if it were beautiful
for miles
and the air mistook the fiery muzzle blasts
for some misunderstood intelligence from God
and quieted the place for prayer.

But
afterwards there were always saws enough
ranked in the surgeon's mind for the size and toughness
of each shattered bone.
And the screams were such opinions
of grief and pain
that answered the warring rang of metal teeth
that made a repetitious huss
below the meat of arms
dropping like apple branches pruned
to feed the coming fruit
of these young men.

Though listening could not confirm
this possibility from such close vantage
as was had by those in the haunted shade
of their remove
yet
listed and eventual
they had their proof
in the perpetual absence of those who'd died
in the heart of that great and visible noise.

The Day the War Came to Ashbourne, Derbyshire

for Tom Wardlaw

Tom said the Albemarle was a dud
famous for falling from the sky
like a shot duck.
Without provocation
it would drop through cloud cover
and ram its naked shadow
down the runnels of a valley
or over the rooftops of a village
busy with the morning.

But on that day
the day remembered as
the day the war came to Ashbourne, Derbyshire
no one could have guessed it
as they flew lumbering back
in the dark, miles from the front
on a training run in '44
flying low so they hit the house
at two-hundred-and-fifty miles an hour.
Hit it hard so the sky ship
crumpled and shrieked on the brick's
exploding walls
taking Danny from his chart table
and hurling him in a crush
like a Camberwell beauty
flung without the usual fritillary
of a blow to the head.
Out of the darkness into a deeper darkness
that makes of this newlywed
an unsurprisable and ugly lump.
And the pilot shot unmarked
by the ballistics
of a snout that penetrates

deep into the English domicile
reducing the air foil to a redundant shudder
as the fuselage
settles with a groan and fractures into torn sections
that smash the fly-boys' faces
into rude and open horrors
that would never heal.

Seven months they were
stunned to the hospital sheets.
Seven months until they told them
Danny had died
smoothing the maps to find home.
His last thought travelling
down his fingertips to the network
scrawled upon the grid
till he flung against the fence
that drifted him in cut sections
like a cheese knife.

Not for forty years did they learn why
and the reason
trivialized their being
so they shrank to their scars
stung and meaningless.
The pilot had failed to reset a switch
so simple and significant as a last breath.
So they flew in low
like an owl after rabbit
their tricycle carriage hoisted
into its skirts.
And they measured time
shaving seconds into clipped slivers
so their collapsing panoramas
shot up in still unfractured rectangles

peeling each instant into pitiless exposures
that pitched in the mind
like screaming sheets of tin.

Their dream is to return to the glittering instant
before in the sleepy night
when the darkness hung on their plane
like a cage
and to reset life
to an unpunished tramp through the air
that would lift their shattered bird
backwards through its mended flight
and either kill them like heroes
or leave them yawning in the hanger
with the ennui of all disgruntled men
who take life for granted.

Playing Chess with God

I reach for my piece
and it withers
like pipe smoke threading my hand.
It is but a fragrance of its former self.
A stick of burnt incense
it turns to ash and dissipates.
"Your move. Your move. Your move."
He says, an ebbing benediction
palming a pawn each time
with the ease of a riverboat gambler
one tooth flashing gold.
I watch them go
these lost loves
diminished in His palm.
He likes His bishops best.
Favours their diagonal slide
prefers it to the chorus-girl kick of the knight
the unnecessary honesty of rooks
or the hubris of the orgulous queen
who scatters jackals like a gunshot in the air.
He throws a guard of grace around His corrupted king
dethrones my own
then says, "The game's not over yet.
Your move, your move, your move..."

When Johnny Swam

I was having breakfast with God.
He had bacon and eggs (sunny side up).
I had wafers and wine.
He said
His favourite actor
was Johnny Weissmuller.
He said
His favourite song
was Johnny's Tarzan yell.
"Oh, the way he could call
the great-tusked bull elephants
in from the Savannah
to smash the village
and trample the Pygmies."
God looked a little hurt,
but He finished simply
"When Johnny swam
he swam like an angel."
and playing His fork
through broken yolk, God said
"When Johnny swam
I had faith in man."

Hired Man in Paradise

Tom is scything nettles
in the pine grove again.
Even though his bones are laid out
forever
like a Sunday suit
in a gray box
he still wades in
a coverall reckoning.
More black fly than angel.
Smiling like a running dog.
This is his heaven:
To rap a hog snout so it thunks.
To switch the rump of a slow-moving cow.
He's married the task;
made a bride of labour
where flung wheat sheaves hover
like Seraphim
and a sickle
makes a weird Gabriel
beneath the smoke-ring halo of a Trump cigar.

Confessions of a Body Breaking Down

I'd known him for eleven years
and in all that time
I'd never heard him speak my name.
Never had so much as a single conversation
with the man
save the morning, "Yup"
when he passed me in the hall
the acoustics of his salutation like a belch...
that is, until he became diabetic.
Now he stretches his lean frame out
arranging his bones on the couch
like a tired old dog on a bed of stones.
And there he begins to hold forth
on his disease.
Dithyrambs on the wonders of dizzy spells
and the many virtues
of the common orange
and the celebration of a pain-filled night
when you know you are alive
sustaining a house of flesh for the agony within
for the Cartesian, "I ache, therefore I am!"
and the blue needle pricks that fleck
the back of his knee.
And the expert inventory of moods.
And the sugar levels rising and falling
in his system like the traces of a bad drug.
And the weight loss that makes him hit
another notch in his belt with a nail,
or fold his brown trousers over in front
like a kind of ugly unresolved origami.
And so he speaks
until he convinces us
that the climate of his body
is an unrelenting drizzle
a skyful greyness that validates his being

and makes him talk
as if a gun were being held to his head—
talk like a radio flicking round the bands.

And still he never speaks my name.
As if it were a curse.
As if it might cure his malediction
and leave him with nothing to say
nothing to do
but pull and stroke
the pucker of flesh beneath his chin.

How to Put an Old Dog Down

Once upon a porch...

there was a man who had an old dog
and the dog, being old,
had decided not to die
though he did nothing
but lie waiting, suffering the hours—
so the man, loving his dog,
decided to put him down.

And, being kind,
he considered and rejected
a litany of cruel options
for this brisk resolve—
Yes, he had decided
to dynamite the dog.

And, carrying the poor old fellow,
for he could not walk,
to the edge of the trees
beyond the house
he strapped the dog with TNT
so he lay like a canine car bomb
fizzing by the lit fuse.

And, the man, turning,
walked towards the house
keening for his lost pet.

But Dogod was up to His old monkey business
and He revived the smitten mutt
who rose and frolicked in his fashion after his master
dragging the fuse line
like a burning leash.

And the man, being no fool,
picked up the pace,
as did his faithful pooch,
and so on
until the fellow
hit the porch with a leap
and was overthewelcomematandintothehouse
behindtheboltedoordashingpastthekitchen
forthesanctuaryofthebackshed(breathless) when
the hound
made the porch at a gallop
as if this were some game
half-remembered from his puppyhood
as a sudden and brutal blast
ripped through the house
sending shock waves
rippling across the field
and bringing shingles, and bits of dog
twisting down through the tree tops
the dog's nose intact
still snapping at squirrel smells
while it fell.

Why Some People Retire

for Roger

When Gill Golightly
cut his fingers in with the chops
he sawed them through
like a carpenter
jigging nails in with the wood
so they sat
in the butcher's paper
like cigar stubs thrown away lit
and he held them high
for Mrs. Quinn
poked in the meat.
The stroke had cut the circuit
in his bad arm
so the first surprise
when he held high the mess and said,
"Take a look at these babies."
was Mrs. Quinn
keeling backwards in a senseless thud
like a broom handle.
Still, the nonplussed Golightly
leaning over the counter
didn't know what the fuss was about
till Jonesy coming in said,
"Gill, you've gone and sawed off
yer fingers!"

And so Gill,
looking at his hand
the end of it angled
like panpipes
decided finally to retire.

The Art of Walking Backwards

You thought you understood
the art of walking backwards.

The way the ground turns to air
at the cliff edge.

The way stones feel
against the heel.

The way the rock face
might slam the spine against a jut.

The way window glass
shatters around you
in a dangerous puzzle of cutting reflections.

The way the doorway stays in its joists
or a tree clings shivering to its roots.

The way thin ice gives over deep water
or the swamp sucks you in slowly
like a dropped stone.

One more step
and you will be beyond the verge
free falling
with gulls in the canyon.